Beginners Guide for African Cichlid Success

Easy step by step instructions for setting up a beginners aquarium

By Craig Wrightson

3 simple steps and 10 easy to follow Rules to Success to get most out of your new aquarium guaranteed!

TABLE OF CONTENTS

Introduction 3

What you can expect to learn from this guide: 4

    STEP 1 – RESEARCH 7

    STEP 2 - TANK SET-UP AND PREPARATION 13

    REQUIRED FILTRATION 14

    SUBSTRATE 18

    WATER TEMPERATURE 20

    AERATION and WATER MOVEMENT 22

    ORNAMENTS and ROCKS 24

    LIGHTING 26

    PH and HARDNESS 28

    ECO-SYSTEM 30

    STEP 3 – ADDING FISH 32

Feeding 35

How often should I feed my fish? 37

Common Causes of Death in Aquariums 38

SUMMARY 40

RULES 41

WELCOME TO THE WONDERFUL WORLD OF AFRICAN CICHLIDS!

INTRODUCTION

First and foremost I would like to say Hello and thank-you for purchasing this guide. My name is Craig Wrightson and I have been keeping African Cichlids for about 12 years now and one of the main things I have learnt is that the more effort and time you put into keeping these wonderful fish, the more enjoyment you will get out of watching them thrive.

Over the years I have tried my hand at a number of different species of fish including;

- American Cichlids also known as New World Cichlids, including *Oscars* and the mighty *Jack Dempsey*.

- South American Tropical's such as *Discus*, *Cardinal Tetras* and *Angel Fish* just to name a few of many.

- Tropical fish from around the Globe like the *Dwarf Gourami* from India

- *Betas* and even the humble *Gold Fish*.

I can say this, even after keeping all those different fish, African Cichlids always manage to win me back. They have everything a fish handler looks for, vibrant colour, always active and because of their huge genus there is always going to be a fish for any level of experience from the beginner all the way up to an expert.

They are an extremely rewarding animal to keep, I find that no matter how stressed, worried or bothered I may be feeling or no matter how tough my day has been, sitting down and watching these fish is a sure fire way to cheer me up.

I hope that I will be able to help you benefit from my experience and the knowledge that I have gained over the years. Hopefully by learning from my mistakes, we can get you on a path leading straight to Cichlid Success!!! Of course despite that, you will still likely experience a few bumps along the way but as the old saying goes "one must learn to walk before you can run". So whatever you do don't be tempted to take shortcuts. You need to be patient and you will reap the rewards.

Before we go on it is important to know that if you are a beginner at keeping fish, no matter how well you follow directions and try and do the correct thing, there's a good chance that not everything will go as smoothly as you would like, and you will likely have some set-backs. Be prepared, and look at these as learning opportunities.

By no means am I trying to scare you off, this is just all part of the learning process. Just remember not to let set-backs or mistakes get the best of you and make you give up all together. Once you get bitten by the fish bug, you will appreciate the challenges along with the beauty and relaxation they provide in your home. It is indeed a rewarding hobby that can provide an endless amount of enjoyment, so it is well worth working through and overcoming the difficulties.

WHAT YOU CAN EXPECT TO LEARN FROM THIS GUIDE:

- How to set up a good beginner tank for African Cichlids; a lot of what you will learn in this guide can be applied as good practice when setting up nearly any fresh water aquarium for nearly any fish species.
- Be able to know with confidence, which items you should (and some you shouldn't) buy when setting up a fish tank from scratch.
- Shortcut your learning curve with important hints and tips that I have learned – save you time and money, and keep you from making the common mistakes that can cost you a small fortune.
- What brands, sizes and models I recommend to save you dollars and loads of frustration
- What to do when set-backs occur; it will guide you on how to deal with some of the more common problems known to the aquarium hobbyists as well as provide you with some special tips to help prevent a reoccurrence.

For the sake of trying to make this simple to follow, I am going to break up the whole process into 3 main steps, along with 10 rules to success.

If you are anything like me, then you should find it easier to absorb information in smaller chunks. Hopefully, it will also make for a better read!

Along the way I also list the "10 Rules to success"; take note of these and remember they are there for a good reason ☺. Think of them as a guiding hand and try to do whatever you can to always remember and follow them.

Also, I should mention that I am an Australian and live in Queensland, so this will be relevant to some of the information I have provided. I have attempted to convert and supply information that is relevant for the U.S. So if you happen to notice something that is missing, or that doesn't apply, then please feel free to contact me and I will edit future versions.

Mostly, I hope you get many hours of enjoyment and pleasure over the years to come, looking after your African Cichlids and your home Freshwater Aquarium!

IMPORTANT – *Tip for Beginners!* The entire process of setting up an aquarium is not something you can do in an afternoon or even over a couple of days, the entire process will take around 5 to 6 weeks. This is because fish cannot be added to a new aquarium straight away. So please don't go out and buy lots of fish straight after you have added the water, read this guide through completely, take some notes if you like, but then go through it again.

When you read it the first time you will get an overview of the whole process, and then when you go through the second time you can be taking specific notes or following along with the steps. It is important that you are not expecting to set your tank up one day, and are putting fish in it the next.

ELONGATUS MPANGA

STEP 1 – RESEARCH

OK! Before you throw your hands up in horror, Yes… to many people, research doesn't sound like much fun, but to quote another old saying, *an ounce of prevention is worth a pound of cure!*

When you want to set up a new tank there are a few things that you absolutely need to do before you get underway with all the "exciting and fun stuff". (Yes we do get to that… I promise).

Firstly you need to have a good think about what type of African Cichlids you want to have in your new Aquarium. So you will want to go give Google or your local Aquarium specialist a work over. Here are some basics that will get you started.

RULE #1
A "WELL BALANCED AND HARMONIOUS" TANK WILL GREATLY REDUCE THE CHANCES OF UNHAPPY ENDINGS.

Highly recommended (but by no means a set rule), when setting up a tank, particularly as a beginner, try to choose fish from just one of the below lakes, in other words trying to set up a tank, ergo "well balanced and harmonious"

Here is a bit of background information concerning these amazing fish, there are three main Origins of African Cichlids.
- LAKE MALAWI
- LAKE VICTORIA
- LAKE TANGANYIKA

These lakes are located in Southern Africa situated quite closely together in retrospect of their size. Below is an image showing the 3 great lakes from an image taken by a satellite.

Southern Africa

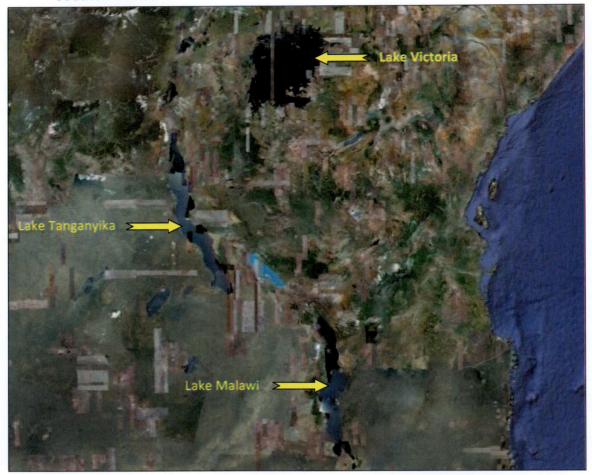

Image courtesy of Google Earth © 2010 TerraMetrics

There are also quite literally thousands of species of African Cichlids, obviously far too many to try and list here. I highly recommend this free website for specific fish information:

[African cichlid genus gallery](#) – if any links don't work, type them into Google.

They go to fantastic lengths to list as many species as possible and to give you a brief rundown about any particular fish you might be interested in. I find this site to be a great resource to have at your fingertips, especially when you are trying to decide what fish will tank well with others.

As mentioned earlier a well balanced and harmonious tank will greatly reduce friction and conflict of ideal water conditions between certain fish that would otherwise live in different environments. A variety of factors vary from one native location to another such as different pH, water hardness and overall temperature of the lakes.

RULE # 2
NOTHING IS SET IN STONE, THERE ARE ALWAYS EXCEPTIONS.

Just like everyday life there are exceptions to the norm, this also being the case for keeping fish. Just because a fish might come from the same lake as the one swimming next to him doesn't mean they are going to be a match made in heaven.

Aggression is a large part of an African Cichlids way of life and unfortunately it is a common issue in Cichlid tanks.

Thankfully aggression can be easily controlled and later on in this guide I will give you some easy tips on helping to keep this problem at bay forever!

For the following exercise we are going to pick 4 common cichlids and see how they could potentially get on together in an aquarium.

So for our example, let's say we have searched on the net, been to a few aquarium shops and found 4 different African Cichlids which we would like to have in our new aquarium.

Tip for Beginners! - I would recommend the following fish for a beginner because of their ease of care and flexibility of water parameters.

You will notice I have also used the common as well as the scientific name.

ELECTRIC BLUE (SCIAENOCHROMIS FRYERI)

ELECTRIC YELLOW (LABIDOCHROMIS CAERULEUS)

BLUE DOLPHIN (CYRTOCARA MOORII)

GIRAFFE CICHLID (NIMBOCHROMIS VENUSTUS)*

Side Note: –* The Giraffe Cichlid has been found to live in all three above mentioned lakes, for this reason I have chosen this fish is because they have great resilience to different water parameters.

1st Question: – where do they all originate from?
Answer: – Lake Malawi

Because they all originate from Lake Malawi and the surrounding area, you can be reasonably sure that the water requirements for all four fish should not differ to the point of concern. That being said please refer to **RULE # 2.**

RULE # 3
ALL AFRICAN CICHLID SPECIES ARE IN SOME WAY AGGRESSIVE OR TERRITORIAL. TAKE STEPS TO MATCH THE LEVEL OF AGGRESSION WITH ALL FISH YOU INTEND TO KEEP.

2nd Question: – what are their temperaments like?
Answer – This is where the above mentioned website comes into play, they list the temperaments of the fish so you can quickly and easily work out what is the likely hood of potential conflict between any of them.
Given that I know these fish all fall under a "semi aggressive" nature, it is fair to say that there shouldn't be too much conflict between the different species, as they are on a par.

3rd Question: – how big are these fish going to grow and will the tank I want to buy or already own do the job?

Answer: – Once again you will find information about the potential maximum size of these fish, at the website I mentioned previously. The fish in question will not likely grow more than 6 inches so they are classed as a medium sized variety.

In regards to the tank size itself, it depends, but is not limited to the following:
- The adult size of the fish you intend to keep
- The quantity of fish you want to keep
- The available space in your home

These fish (based on an average quantity of 3-4 fish per species, so a total of 12 to 16 fish) will have no issues living in a 4ft or 250-300ltr (60-80gal) tank, so from there it's quite simple, the more fish you want the bigger the tank you will need and to some degree the opposite is also true.

Little Helper!
3ft tank = 8-12 fish
4ft tank = 12-16 fish
6ft tank = 16-20 fish
This is a guide only just to help you along the way….remember, *RULE #2!*

As a rule of thumb it is said, that a 4ft tank should be the minimum size to use for most African Cichlids, and I would tend to agree with this, however I have successfully kept Africans in a 3ft tank with no problem, this just meant that I needed to perform a few small water changes a bit more often.

Tip for Beginners! – I wouldn't recommend anything over 4 feet in length, as maintenance, water quality upkeep and overall costs are things that need to be considered. My advice; start off smaller and work your way up!

STEP 2 - TANK SET-UP AND PREPARATION

Now that the research is out of the way, and we have decided on the fish as well as the size tank we want, we can now start to look at getting it ready for its new tenants.

So... just to clarify, at this point you may have a tank, but NOT the fish. There is some work to do before adding your fish, and as tempting as it is, you must get your tank ready well before bringing your new fish home.

The following important points are things that you must understand when you go about setting up your tank.

- REQUIRED FILTRATION
- SUBSTRATE
- WATER TEMPERATURE
- AERATION AND WATER MOVEMENT
- ORNAMENTS AND ROCKS
- LIGHTING
- PH AND HARDNESS
- ECO-SYSTEM

We will go through each of these separately so you know exactly what has to happen to ensure a smooth transition from Aquarium shop to your brand new home tank.

REQUIRED FILTRATION

RULE # 4
YOU CAN'T HAVE TOO MUCH FILTRATION!

African Cichlids love to make a mess. They are always moving substrate around and sifting through the gravel to find bits of leftover food. It's unavoidable and in some cases can be dangerous, but I will touch on that a bit later. (It is also part of what makes them fun and entertaining to watch)

The filter is one of the most important things you need in an aquarium and for this sole reason I strongly suggest that cheaper is NOT better! This is not the place to cut costs.

*Some good brands that I would recommend are Fluval, Sera and Eheim.

Many times I have seen people with cheap and inadequate filtration for their aquarium and more often than not this leads to unhealthy fish due to an imbalance of chemicals within the water caused by poor filtration.

In relation to filtration there a couple of questions you need to ask yourself;

1st Question: – what types of filtration will I need?
Answer:– Two types; firstly, you will need a Canister or "external" filter; these are quite big and for this reason they usually sit under your aquarium, often in an enclosed cupboard, filtering the water through hoses coming out of the top and down the back of your tank. These filters have a high water flow and are the main filter of the tank. Secondly, you will need to have an internal filter; this filter is much smaller and sits on the inner wall of the tank. Its main purpose is to keep the water moving around in the aquarium (emulating a current in a lake or river for example) and at the same time helping with the filtration of your tank.

2nd Question: – what size filters will I need?

Answer: – Over the years I have made a small guide for canister filters to assist with decision making. I have included Litres per hour as well as Gallons per hour.

- 600-800l/h (150-200 g/h) covers a 2-3 foot tank
- 800-1000l/h (200-250g/h) should adequately filter a 4 foot tank without trying too hard
- 1400 -1800l/h (350-400g/h) should cater for a 5-6 foot tank

However while using the above guide as a **guide only;** I follow a very good rule when it comes to the size of filters that I buy.

When I have decided on the brand I want to purchase, for example a Fluval, I find out what model and water flow rates (l/h or g/h) are available, I refer to my guide listed above and then I simply buy the next model up! Of course I only do this where I may think it may be necessary (*explained below*); otherwise sticking to the guide will assure you adequate filtration.

The reason behind this is twofold; (**A**) *RULE # 4* and (**B**) it allows for future upgrades of your tank. Buying a filter that is designed to be able to deal with more water than you have is not at all a bad thing; in fact it could end up saving you a lot of money in the future. I do this for both my canister and internal filters.

Speaking of internal filters, here are a few models that I would recommend for use with a 4 foot tank when paired with a good canister filter, note that each model has different sizes available to suit any size tank you happen to have.

- Eheim aquaball internal filter 2212
- Fluval u4 internal filter
- Sicce shark filter 800 adv

By no means am I saying that you have to buy any of the above models, there are literally hundreds of different types and brands of filters on the market (good and bad) and when the time comes to buy one for yourself than I would suggest having a good chat to your local aquarium shop specialist about the different types they have available, and what they would recommend for your current or future set up.

When you get your new filters home, the best thing to do is to have a good look at the instruction manuals that come with the product straight away. Some of the canister filters especially can be a bit harder than you may think to put together.

Filter Media

More often than not when you buy a filter it will come with everything you need including the entire amount of filter media you require to get underway. Also, depending on what brand and quality of filter you have bought, the quality of the media you are given will also vary.

Generally speaking filter media should be replaced every 4 to 6 months and once again cheaper is not better! There are so many different types of filter media on the market these days it can get very hard for someone new in this hobby to know just what type is the best to buy. I am going to try and make this as simple as possible for you.

I have broken down the process of buying filter media into some simple to follow recommendations.

In my opinion, Seachem produce some of the best filter media on the market today, the following 4 products are strongly recommended to use in any Canister Filter and they are in no particular order:

- MATRIX™ - provides exceptional removal of Ammonia, Nitrite and Nitrate from the aquarium.

- PURIGEN™ - removes soluble and insoluble impurities from water at a rate and capacity that exceeds all others by over 500%, it also aides in the removal of Ammonia, Nitrite and Nitrate.

- MATRIXCARBON™ - It performs better than other top grade carbons by 200-300% when compared for capability to remove organic matter, absorption rate and duration of use.

- FILTRATION FOAM – Some Canister filters require certain shapes of foam to fit the internal segments, this can be very expensive to accommodate however if you buy a sheet of foam you can cut out pieces to fit nearly any canister filter on the market.

I use all 4 of the above media in all my canister filters. With all 4 in your canister filter you will be giving your new fish the best possible chance to be healthy and active for many years.

I would also like to say that good quality Filter Media is not cheap, for this reason I understand the choice of buying cheaper options, especially when first starting out with this hobby (I too have done this). However the lesson to take from here is this; A lot of what I am sharing with you comes from many years of trial and error, by no means am I saying you must go out and buy the products I suggest but if you're in a position to be able to put some money away and save for these items I can say with confidence that you aquarium keeping experience will become easier tenfold.

SUBSTRATE

Substrate is the gravel at the bottom of your tank. It comes in all sorts of types, colours and sizes.

Choosing substrate depends on a couple of things;
- The fish you intend to keep
- Your personal likes and dislikes.

Some African Cichlids like the **FOSSOROCHROMIS ROSTRATUS** commonly called "Rostratus" are sand sifters; they go along the bottom of the tank, sifting the sand through their mouths collecting little bits of food along the way. They also use the sand as a defensive system by burying themselves to the point of being completely out of sight.

On the other hand the **SCIAENOCHROMIS FRYERI** commonly called "Electric Blue" loves to move the substrate around with its mouth to create small creators that he treats as his territory, so for example if you had sand as the substrate for this fish, it would make it a little harder for him to do what he does naturally.

Unfortunately substrate is something that not many people give that much thought too, generally they would see something they like and buy it. However African

Cichlids need a PH level that, in aquatic terms is quite high, anywhere from 7.5 through to 9.5 (More Alkaline than most).

Keeping this in mind substrate can play a bigger role than you may think in what your water PH is going to level out at. Some substrates can actually help raise the PH and "buffer" the level within your tank.

The colour of your substrate in my opinion is not overly important; I honestly believe that it is a personal thing. Some people like fake looking Substrate that is bright in colour and really stands out while others prefer the more natural look of crushed coral for example.

I have seen a lot of conflicting arguments on the internet about this very subject and to some degree I am sure a lot of them have valid points, the general consensus is as follows;

- Darker Substrate tends to bring out the colour of lighter fish
- Lighter Substrate is known to bring out the colour of darker fish

I personally have never had any issue with any colour that I have used in the past. As a general rule, a substrate that helps buffer the PH is going to be lighter in colour.

Size on the other hand, or how coarse the Substrate can be, is something that I find to be reasonably important.

When selecting your new substrate you need to keep in mind the cleaning and maintenance of it. I find that if you choose something that is really fine like sand for example, cleaning can be quite difficult. This is due to the particles being so small they tend to just get sucked straight up with the water in your gravel cleaner and you end up with a bucket half full of sand. Another point to be wary of is the sand being sucked up into your filters, this being something to avoid.

Tip for Beginners! - My preferred choice would be a medium grade substrate, I find that this level of coarseness not only looks great but is a lot easier to maintain and keep clean. Of course this means I only keep fish that suit this particular environment, so the "Rostratus" cichlid that loves sand is not one that I keep in my tank.

The best thing to do when getting your substrate would be to ask your local aquarium shop if they stock any Calcium Carbonate Substrate or Crushed Coral, these will greatly improve your tanks ability in keeping the pH within the correct range.

WATER TEMPERATURE

The water temperature is critical, because it not only affects a fish's health, but also contributes to future breeding and algae control. Because of where I live (Queensland Australia) the water temperature can become extremely hard to manage in summer, this is due to everyday temperatures exceeding 30°c (86°F), I will share some easy examples of keeping your tank cool in summer if you live in a similar environment.

The ideal temperature for an African tank can vary slightly from species to species however if you are unsure of the ideal temperature for the fish you have chosen, then a safe average is approximately 26-28°c (78-82°F). I would also like to point out that the website I mentioned earlier in the guide tells you the ideal temperature range for its entire library of fish!

Cooling

A mentioned earlier the Australian summer can get quite difficult to keep the temperature of the tank bellow 30°c (86°F), I have had many frustrating times trying to work out the best way to keep the tank cool in summer without having to spend a fortune on cooling equipment.

The only sure fire to keep your tank at a set temperature day in and day out is to get a "water chiller". This is typically used by people for Marine Aquariums due to their critical nature of temperature control.

The only set back is their cost, they tend to get quite expensive, especially for the good brands and before you know it you're looking at having to spend in excess of $1,000.

I personally keep my tanks safe from "heat spikes" in summer by adding ice to the tank in small amounts as to not drop the temp too quickly but to stop any severe rise that might happen through a hot day; this however can get tricky especially when you're not home for example.

I know that this might sound odd and I know that a lot of people would question it but hey, if something works for you, then do it!

NOTE – using ice to cool your tank can be dangerous if not done properly. A sudden drop of water temperature opens the door to things like white spot which all the while being easily treatable still has the potential to cause great issues and even death in your aquarium. Given this I would highly recommend the following ways to keep the tanks temperature down in summer for a beginner.

The position of your tank in your house can play a big role, such as making sure it is not in direct sunlight, also that it is in a fairly large room, preferably one that is well insulated. These simple measures can help slow your tanks heating rate in summer. Another way of course, is if you have air conditioning in your home, then you can set it to 24°c (75°F) and keep the house at an overall nice temp which basically will prevent your fish tank getting too hot.

Heating

Keeping your tank within the desired temperature range, year round, especially during the winter months will require a water heater. When purchasing your aquarium water heater you will need to make sure that you get one that is capable of heating the quantity of water in your tank.

There are a lot of different types of water heaters on the market. If we take the rule of thumb again with a 4ft tank as a standard minimum size, you will need a heater that is capable of heating the whole tank which holds around 250lt or 75 gals.

A 150 – 200W is more than sufficient to heat most any common 4ft tank on the market and prices do vary quite a lot between brands. Once again, the bigger the tank the more watts you will need and vice versa.

Here is a small guide;
- 100 – 150W should suit a 3 foot tank
- 150 – 200W should suit a 4 foot tank
- 250 – 300W should suit a 6 foot tank

With a heater it's my opinion that it is not necessary to spend big bucks to get top brands when you first start out, in all honesty they can get quite expensive and unless money is no object I can't see any real need to get the best brands straight away.

I have found the cheaper ones to work quite well. What I will mention is the old saying *'you get what you pay for'* still rings true. What I have noticed with the cheaper brands, although they work just fine, their working life is shorter. . Putting it simply, the cheaper it costs, the sooner you will need to replace it!

AERATION and WATER MOVEMENT

RULE # 5
WITH NO OXYGEN NOTHING WILL SURVIVE!

For your new tank you will need an air pump and air stone, in fact for a 4ft tank I would strongly recommend buying a pump that can accommodate two air stones.

Air pumps come in all types and they usually have 1 – 2 outlets although I have seen a pump with eight on it once. The best thing about air pumps is that they are easy and straight forward, if you want to run two air stones, buy a pump with two outlets then you know it's going to run two stones with no problem.

Beginners Tip - Keeping your Air pump elevated is definitely recommended, this is mainly because of the risk of power outages. In some cases when a black out occurs it can start a chain reaction due to the laws of gravity. While your Air Pump is working it is forcing air into the water, if this suddenly stops the water can force its way back through the Air Stone and siphon out through the pump and onto the floor. Keeping you Air pump elevated is a good way to counteract this potential problem.

Having air pumping into your tank is vital to the survival of your fish; if this fails (including power outages) given enough time your fish will exhaust all the oxygen in the water, and while this might sound strange, they will suffocate and die. The more fish in your tank, the quicker the oxygen is used, the less time they have.

Avoiding the problem of power outages, or black-outs is difficult but by no means impossible. There are some things you can do, and being prepared ahead of time, for such things is a wise move.

Of course as with most things, your solution will depend on your budget. There are basically three options.

1st Option: Also the most affordable option is battery a powered air pump. These are readily available on eBay and similar websites; they may also be more readily available in the US or the UK. Keeping two of these stored for such an occasion is definitely a great solution, the only real drawback to this option is of course you would have to make sure you are home if a power outage occurred and obviously that is easier said than done.

2nd Option: Get a Power Generator. This can be quite expensive not to mention noisy, however, the benefit of having your own power generator is not only can you run your air pump; you can also run your whole tank and maybe even some other things in your household, depending on the size of the generator you purchase.

3rd Option: You get a UPS or "uninterrupted power supply", these are fantastic, but once again they are a little pricy when you do the research. They run completely silent and are very easy to keep hidden out of the way, the only down side you have with a UPS is that they only last for a few hours anywhere from 4-8 maybe a bit more depending on the model purchased. So obviously this option would only be beneficial for short term outages.

ORNAMENTS and ROCKS

RULE # 6
FISH NEED PLACES TO HIDE!

If you're going to keep African Cichlids, you are going to need to get a hold of some rocks and ornaments to put in the tank. Cichlids just love to swim in and out of the rocks and little fish need places to hide for their protection from the larger fish.

A recommended rock is the volcanic rock or any porous rock that has big holes throughout it that the fish can hide in and swim through. See above picture.

In saying that, by no means do you need that specific kind of rock, just so long as you can position the rocks you do have, in a manner that will give your fish places to hide for protection as well as provide little homes for them. Creating small caves for your fish is important, however there are some things you need to be aware of when setting up your rocks.

Earlier on in this guide I mentioned how Africans love to move substrate around with their mouths and sometimes this can be dangerous, well this is where we will cover how that can be a problem.

The way you stack your rocks is very important, let's say you leave a rock balancing precariously on the top edge of another and overnight one of your fish decides to move some substrate that is below the rock that's supporting the top rock. This could lead to a number of issues which could be catastrophic for your fish, your tank and indeed even your home.

The rock that is sitting on top may move, slip off and if big enough could crack the glass in your tank. Clearly the ramifications of this happening could be dreadful.

The best way to prevent this is to make sure that when you stack your rocks you make them as sturdy as possible, a good way to do this is by giving them a little bit of a shake and wobble once you have placed them.

If they tend to tilt and move easily than readjust them so they are sturdy where they sit. This will help prevent any potential issues that the fish may cause with substrate movement, not having as much of an impact on nearby stacked rocks.

Another way to provide protection for your fish, as well as improve the aesthetics of your tank, is to get some aquarium plants. In my opinion there are no major benefits to any particular variety of plant. I find the best way to get plants is to look for the ones you like the look of and buy them!

I should clarify here, that I am not in any way an expert on aquarium plants, and it is quite possible some plants produce different effects or chemical changes in the water. I don't think that there are any significant changes when using any of the main plant varieties available through the majority of your local aquarium retailers. So for the purpose of this work, I don't believe there is anything that would impact significantly when setting up a beginner's tank.

Tip for Beginners! – If you really like the thought of having some plants in with your fish, try getting your hands on some plastic plants. Now days they are very realistic and as a bonus they won't ever die or rot.

NOTE - If you would like to learn more about creating and caring for the Planted Aquarium please visit this free website,
http://www.plantedtank.net/articles

LIGHTING

RULE # 7
Not just any light will do!

Lighting is another factor that is very important for the health of your fish. When you take a look at all the different types of lighting available it can become quite daunting.

The idea of lighting an aquarium is to simulate the sun, this doesn't mean just grab any old light and go for it, because unfortunately the common household fluorescent bulb does not produce the right colour or the right heat for your tank.

There are a lot of different things that the light does and it all depends on the type of spectrum that the particular light produces. Different fish react differently depending on what spectrum of light you buy.

Lighting can also become quite complicated, the more experience you have in keeping fish; it gets to the point of where you need to have different types of lighting for different kinds of fish, particularly if you plan to get into breeding fish, and of course this can also become quite expensive.

Tip for Beginners! – Due to the complex nature of this particular topic I think it would be best and easier to recommend a complete lighting set up, something that will give you the basic requirements of a standard 4 foot tank.

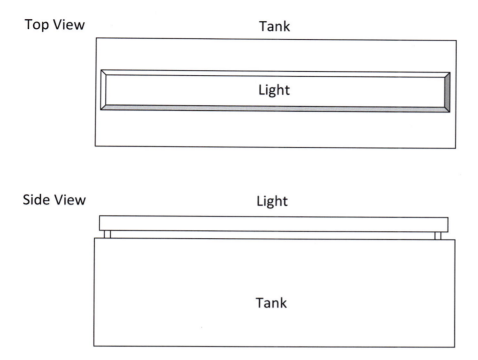

Some lights come with their own little stands that hold them nicely above the tank, others don't. Depending on your tank set up will depend on how the light is fitted, if you have a hood, the light will simply site inside it. If you're like me and have tanks without hoods than you need to be able to sit the light on a bracket that lifts it about 2 inches above the top of the tank.

For a 4 foot tank I suggest to buy a double T8 Fluorescent light (explained further down) that accommodates 2 individual tubes or 2 single T8 lights each with their own tubes, buying the correct size is easy, 4 foot tank = 4 foot light, 3 foot = 3 foot light and so on.

When buying the light from your local aquarium shop just explain that you intend to keep African Cichlids, their recommendation for the correct light will be more than adequate.

A T8 light is going to cover a broad spectrum and be utilised in an all-rounder set-up, as described above. However another very good and highly recommended all rounder light is what they call a T5 light and is simply one of the best types of globes you can buy. You should be able to hunt down a T5 light from your local aquarium without any problems or failing that, remember EBay☺.

The one drawback to the T5 is its general cost, they are not cheap but I can say with confidence that the money you spend on your light will be well worth it.

By no means do you have to go with a T5, there are lots of other lighting options including the T8, this type of light is a little bit more common within the industry due to its low cost, especially when comparing to the T5. It looks a lot like a standard fluorescent tube you would commonly see in someone's house though usually they have a red or pink colour to them. So depending on your situation it might pay to look around and ask what types of lighting your aquarium shop stocks and compare them.

NOTE – Beware of imitation T5 lights selling on the internet, my advice is this, if it seems too good to be true it probably is (yes, sadly this is even true with keeping fish).

Below is a link to an article which describes a lot better than I ever could, the workings of the fluorescent bulbs and the full light spectrum, it is a very interesting read and I highly recommend it.

A FREE ARTICLE ON AQUARIUM LIGHTING CAN BE FOUND HERE,
http://www.mchportal.com/fishkeeping

This article burrows deep into the heart of the lighting requirements and should be able to answer any questions you may have.

PH and HARDNESS

Keeping your tank at the right pH is again another critical factor, even though some genus of African Cichlids can tolerate a relative wide range of pH, it is always good practice to keep it as stable as possible.

pH can be detrimental to your fish's health. If the water in your tank is kept too acidic or alkaline for a more than a couple of weeks it will have adverse effects on their wellbeing, ultimately leading to the death of your fish.

So as we are at the stage of adding water to our new tank, this is the perfect time to discuss the issues of pH. Once you have decided on what you are going to put in your tank in the way of gravel, ornaments and rocks, you will now need to fill your tank with water. This is literally as easy as getting a garden hose and filling up your tank with it. Of course you can use buckets; however this does take a considerably longer time to do.

Now that your tank is filled with tap water, the next step you will need to do is test your water for the following things;

Following is a list of each lake with its specific pH range and Hardness levels.

- lake Malawi ph range from 7.8 to 8.6 and 6 to 8 dh (degrees of hardness)
- lake Tanganyika ph range from 8.6 to 9.5 and 11 to 17 dh
- lake Victoria ph range from 7.2 to 8.6 and 2 to 8 dh

Ok, time to spend more money ☺ (I hope you are taking notes BEFORE you go to the store).

This will require a water test kit. Just like everything else, Test Kits come in all shapes sizes and prices ranges, offering different testing abilities along the way.

The above 3 chemicals, are definitely not the only ones you will need to test for and monitor in your tank, however they are the most important as far as getting your new tank underway with the correct water parameters.

I recommend getting a good quality test kit that covers the following;
- AMMONIA ($NH_3 + NH_4$)
- NITRITE (NO^2)
- NITRATE (NO^3)
- PH (HIGH AND LOW RANGE)
- GENERAL WATER HARDNESS (GH)

If you are unable to find a single test kit that covers all of the above, more often than not you will be able to buy individual test packages.

As an example *Sera* provide a very good starter test kit which can be easily added to by buying separate individual test kits. Check at your local aquarium shop to see what they keep in stock.

Seachem produce a range of products that I find are the best to help keep my tanks at the right pH and Hardness for all the cichlids that I keep.

Two particularly good products, I recommend are **Seachem Malawi/Victoria Buffer** and **Tanganyika Buffer** both of which are formulated to increase hardness and maintain pH for optimum replication of the corresponding lake environments.

If these are not available in your local aquarium store than I highly recommend buying them online if you have the means to do so.

ECO-SYSTEM

RULE # 8
PATIENCE IS A VIRTUE (ESPECIALLY KEEPING FISH… ADDED BENEFIT… DEVELOPS CHARACTER ☺)!

When you're setting up a new tank it is extremely important that you let the tank "Cycle" before introducing any fish, this can take anywhere between 4-6weeks and is **ABSOLUTELY NECESSARY**!

To cycle your tank you need to have it filled with water and all the filters connected, running and circulating the water, this means that once you have everything set up and the tank is ready to go, you simply turn everything on.

This gives the water an opportunity to age in the tank removing all the nasty bacteria and replacing it with good bacteria that the fish need to be happy and healthy. In short it is necessary to their survival.

The key however is giving it a head start to generate these good bacteria and time to establish the desirable eco-system that your fish will need to survive and hopefully to thrive.

To do this you will need to purchase some "water ager", this is available at all aquarium shops.

There are quite a few different types of water ager on the market and choosing one can be confusing, especially at first., They all say they do similar if not the same thing and the prices really don't vary all that much from one brand to another.

The best advice I can give here, is to ask your local aquarium what they have in the way of water conditioner for setting up **new tanks**. I recommend a brand called "CYCLE" I have used this for years when setting up a new tank, and I find it works really well plus offers some extras that other brands seem to lack.

The steps for preparing your tank to start establishing this "eco-system" are as follows;

- First you will need to add your conditioner. The instructions for use will always be on the package or the bottle itself, follow the directions and add the correct amount to your new tank.

Tip for beginners! – If you're unsure of the correct volume of your new tank, follow this link and fill out the empty sections for either Gallons or Litres - Volume Calculator

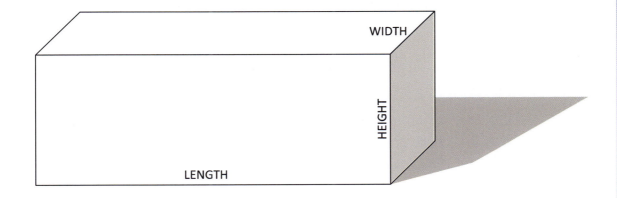

- Second, you **MUST** let your tank sit for a minimum of four weeks (I would strongly recommend five or six) to really give it a chance to get those good bacteria growing. Now you're probably thinking that this is a bit of a low blow and the last thing you want to have to do is look at an empty tank for four weeks however I can't stress enough how important this part of the process is, to your new fish's wellbeing and your ultimate success. The difference is quite literally between happy fish and dead fish.

OK, so at this stage it has been at least four or preferably more weeks and by now your tank should have a nice solid base of good bacteria growing in the filters and water all ready for the third step!

STEP 3 – ADDING FISH

After the 4 or 5 weeks of cycling your tank it's finally time to add some fish but you can't just put all the fish you want in there at once. You start by putting only two or three fish into the new tank to begin with and slowing introducing more fish over the next 3 to 4 weeks

The reason why we add fish to the tank slowly is because your new tank does not have a strong enough eco-system capable of handling anymore than three or four fish at the beginning stages and introducing fish slowly will build up the eco-system to be nice and strong.

Introducing a lot of fish at once will have the opposite effect on the eco-system and will begin to destroy all the good work you have done.

A few things you need to know when buying and adding fish to your aquarium;
- Don't buy too many at once
- Always buy active fish
- Beware of Health and signs of disease

Again... Don't buy too many at once!

Buying too many fish at once can cause unneeded stress on the "Eco-System" as mentioned earlier. Even if your tank has been set up for months or even years and is stable in its chemical balance a large change in fish quantity is enough to throw this balance out and in doing so opens the door for a number of issues including Nitrite/Nitrate poisoning resulting from a large "Bio-Load" within the filter systems.

Secret to Success tip! - Always buy active fish!

Make sure that the fish you want looks happy, seems hungry and very active! For instance if the fish you are looking at in the aquarium shop isn't really swimming around and/or doesn't show any interest in getting fed when you near the tank, then it's a fair chance that something is not quite right with that fish.

Beware of Health and disease... Signs to look for!

The belly of the fish is a great way to see if that fish has had a stressful time and has not been eating. The way to tell this is by the shape of its belly, if it's sinking up into the body in any way, then you know that the fish is malnourished and is not feeding properly. The line of the belly should run straight along the base of its body with no signs of sinking.

The belly does not want to be bloated either; especially if you notice the fish is sitting quietly and not moving around much.

Another health sign to look for is the overall colour, you need to make sure that the fish is sowing nice colouration throughout his body, it does not have to be breeding colouration, (*some cichlids produce wonderful colours when trying to spawn*) but it must be strong enough to see clearly, if the fish is pale or "greyed out" this is also a sign of an unhappy fish.

There are a few reasons why a fish might not be boasting his full body colour. It might be due to the fish having just been relocated to a new tank; however this should only be a temporary thing and should not last long if the fish is healthy and happy.

In regards to diseases the most common would be "White Spot" or "Ich". This is very easily diagnosed due to the fish being covered in tiny white spots all over its body and fins. If you see any fish with this disease DO NOT buy it or any other fish that is in the same tank. WHITE SPOT IS HIGHLY CONTAGIOUS and if brought home to your own aquarium it will quickly take hold and spread to every fish you own.
However!

If you do happen to get a case of White Spot within you aquarium do not panic! There are some very effective remedies for this common disease available either online or at your local aquarium shop. One particular product I would recommend is **WATERLIFE PROTOZIN FISH MEDICATION.** Follow the easy instructions on the container and White Spot will be a thing of the past.

Tip for beginners! – Always try to keep an eye out for White Spot; the sooner it is picked up the easier it is to treat (more on this later).

Follow these basic, yet very important "Key" steps when buying your fish and I guarantee it will greatly increase the survival rate when you finally get them home.

So remember NEVER buy a sick fish, chances are they will not recover from the stress they have endured and sadly these fish will most likely die within a short space in time.

When you bring home, or any new fish to add to your tank, you will need to "float" the fish. This is simply placing the bag that you brought the fish home in, directly into the tank and letting it float in the water. Leave it sealed at this point and then after about 10min undo the bag and place about 2 cups of your aquarium water into the bag, and let the bag sit in the water for another 10min, once the 20min has past it should be reasonably safe to let your new fish free into his new home.

We do the "floating" process to help introduce any fish to a new environment with as little stress to its body as possible. As you may be aware the water in your local aquarium shop is going to be slightly different to your home tank and in doing this we are keeping the fish relaxed or as stress free as possible.

Another point to keep in mind here, if you are adding fish to your tank where there are fish who have established their territory. If you notice they are being aggressive to the newcomers, particularly if they are picking on one, then you might want to net up the bully temporarily.

This can help the new fish get use to the new environment without getting picked on straight away, after about 15 to 20min let the netted fish out again and monitor their behaviour.

FEEDING

RULE # 9
VARIETY IS THE SPICE OF LIFE!

When feeding your African Cichlids, keep them on their toes by feeding them different foods, Variety really is the spice of life! This will be explained further on.

I think it would be best to start by giving you some information as to what types African Cichlids are categorized into. The thing to remember here when learning is that each group has its own unique dietary needs:

- HERBIVOROUS: These fish are grazers and feed by scraping algae off different surfaces within your tank.

- CARNIVOROUS: These fish feed on other fish; they are especially fond of the fry of other species.

- MICRO-PREDATORS: These fish eat small invertebrates such as Artemia and Plankton.

- OMNIVOROUS: These fish have a variety in their diet, eating plant matter, invertebrates, and small fish.

Understanding what group your fish belongs to is very important. The [Cichlid Genus Gallery](#) which I mentioned earlier in this guide will tell you what category your fish falls into.

For example, the Tropheus species from Lake Tanganyika belong to the *herbivorous* group, feeding them lots of frozen bloodworm, or even flake food high in fish meal would not be a good idea and may well end up causing "Bloat", a condition that is very hard to treat and unfortunately more often than not fatal.

Generally speaking the majority of specific African Cichlid food that is on the market is quite well balanced, and provide most of the dietary requirements your fish will need, however there is one thing I think is best left alone.

This would be anything that has beef or ox heart in it. The primary use for these to be added into your fish's food is to unnaturally stimulate growth and in all honesty does more damage than good.

I would like to point out that even though a fish might be herbivorous, they still need a small amount of meat in their diet and same going for carnivorous species needing plant matter, it's all about balance and these should be given to the fish sparingly and viewed like giving your fish a treat say once or twice a every couple of weeks.

A good way to give your carnivorous species a bit of green stuff is to cut a Zucchini into quarters or even a lettuce leaf and throw that into your tank. Fish love this every now and then and benefit a great deal from having it, just remember to wash it before you put it in your tank just to get rid of any nasty chemicals that may have been sprayed onto it (Just like you should when you eat it yourself). ☺

HOW OFTEN SHOULD I FEED MY FISH?

RULE # 10
A HUNGRY FISH IS A HAPPY FISH!

If you have chosen to keep a few different types of Cichlids in your new tank and I would imagine that you have, I would recommend feeding them about 3 times a day. In saying that you must remember that fish need variety so don't give your fish the same type and quantity of food every time, mix it up a bit.

I prefer to give my fish a mix of good quality dry food and a touch of frozen bloodworm, not all at once but spread out over the day and only what they can eat in roughly 30-40 seconds.

Remember not to overfeed your Cichlids, you should leave them wanting more, they are hungry little fish and can eat an amazing amount of food in 30 seconds.

NOTE - A hungry Cichlid is a happy Cichlid see *"RULE #10"*, African Cichlids are well known for their eating ability and from a hobbyist point of view the first sign that something is wrong will be visible in their appetite.

By now hopefully you have two or three fish in the tank and they are happy, healthy and hungry and in a few weeks it will be time to add a couple more.

Handy Tip! - Controlling Aggression!

One of the most common issues I hear about in Cichlid community tanks is the aggression of fish! Thankfully this is something that can be easily controlled.

The major cause for aggression among Cichlids and indeed the majority of animals on Earth is food. By following the basic outline given above, you will find that your new community tank will start to be less aggressive naturally. This is because there will be no need to compete for food.

Also keep in mind the isolation technique I mentioned before. You can do this simply by having a small breeding net. You can place the aggressive fish in there for about 10 to 20 mins. This mainly applies to when you are adding new fish.

COMMON CAUSES OF DEATH IN AQUARIUMS

Ammonia poisoning

This is one of the most common problems that newly set up aquariums face. Also, this can easily occur:
- In a well established tank if too many new fish have been added at once,
- When a filter stops working due to mechanical failure or power failure,
- If there is a sudden change in your tanks Eco-System due to the use of some medications.

Possible Symptoms:
- Fish appear to gasp for air at the water surface
- Purple/red gills
- Fish seem lethargic
- Loss of appetite
- Red streaks running down the fins or body

Potential Treatment:
- Drop the pH below 7.0 (use pH down available from your local aquarium shop)
- 25 - 50% water change
- Use an Ammonia Neutralizer
- Reduce feeding to once every 2 days until Ammonia level is Zero

Nitrite poisoning

Also called *"brown blood disease"*, this horrible poisoning turns the blood of fish brown from a build up of "Methemoglobin" within your tank.

Worst still, Methemoglobin causes the blood to be unable to carry oxygen, which in turn causes suffocation even if there is generous amounts of oxygen within in the water.

Possible Symptoms:
- Fish appear to gasp for air at the water surface
- Fish appear lazy
- Brown gills
- Fast gill movement

Potential Treatment:
- 50% water change
- Add Aquarium salt, use the recommended dosage for your tank on the container
- Reduce feeding to once every 2 days until Nitrite level is Zero
- Increase the aeration

White Spot (Ich)

Think of this disease as being the equivalent of a skin infection, it is easily treatable though keep in mind that it can easily be fatal to a fish.

Fish that have become infected end up being covered with small white spots. Large or severe outbreaks are easy to spot, but the start of this condition often goes unnoticed.

Definite Symptoms:
- Small white spots covering the entire fish's body
- Fish eventually become very lethargic
- Red streaks on the body of the fish in situations of a severe breakout

Potential Treatment:
- Raise the water temperature to above 30°c (86°F)
- Medicate for 1 to 2 weeks (be sure to read instructions concerning fish without scales i.e. Clown Loach)
- Remove active carbon from any filter that is attached to the tank during treatment

SUMMARY

Congratulations, you have now finished the Beginners Guide to African Cichlid Success. For some of you setting up an aquarium can be a pretty daunting task and I hope that this guide has broken down all the information into a digestible manner as to make this process as simple as 1, 2, and 3.

We have covered the basic essentials for setting up your African Cichlid aquarium to the point where we can actually start adding fish and begin to enjoy these wonderful animals in all their fishy goodness.

You might be wondering if I am getting some form of hand out from all the brands/companies that I have mentioned throughout this guide. Far from the truth, I would like to say that the only reason why any brand or company that receives mention, does so because I genuinely believe that they provide the best product concerning the topic in mention.

We have touched on the importance of 8 main requirements for setting up your Tropical Cichlid fish tank:

- REQUIRED FILTRATION
- SUBSTRATE
- WATER TEMPERATURE
- AERATION AND WATER MOVEMENT
- ORNAMENTS AND ROCKS
- LIGHTING
- PH AND HARDNESS
- ECO-SYSTEM

We have also covered 10 Rules to Success for you to always keep in mind and do your best to follow:

RULES

- *RULE #1* - A "well balanced and harmonious" tank will greatly reduce the chances of unhappy endings.
- *RULE # 2* - Nothing is set in stone, there are ALWAYS exceptions.
- *RULE # 3* - All African Cichlid species are in some way aggressive or territorial. Take steps to match the level of aggression with all fish you intend to keep.
- *RULE # 4* - You CAN'T have too much filtration!
- *RULE # 5* - With no oxygen nothing will survive!
- *RULE # 6* - Fish need places to hide!
- *RULE # 7* - Not just any light will do!
- *RULE # 8* - Patience is a virtue (especially keeping fish... added benefit... develops character☺)!
- *RULE # 9* - Variety is the Spice of Life!
- *RULE # 10* - A Hungry Fish is a Happy Fish!

If you follow this guide, don't take short cuts and remember the 10 Rules to Success I can guarantee you will reap great rewards for all your hard work. Keeping fish of any sort is a long term decision, it will also be a never ending learning curve that will keep you on your toes at the times you least expect it too.

I hope that my knowledge can bring you just as much if not more enjoyment as myself from the – Wonderful world of African Cichlids!

Printed in Great Britain
by Amazon